AF408414

HOW TO TIE A BOWTIE WITH PAWLAVARD

A DOG WITH CLASS

King

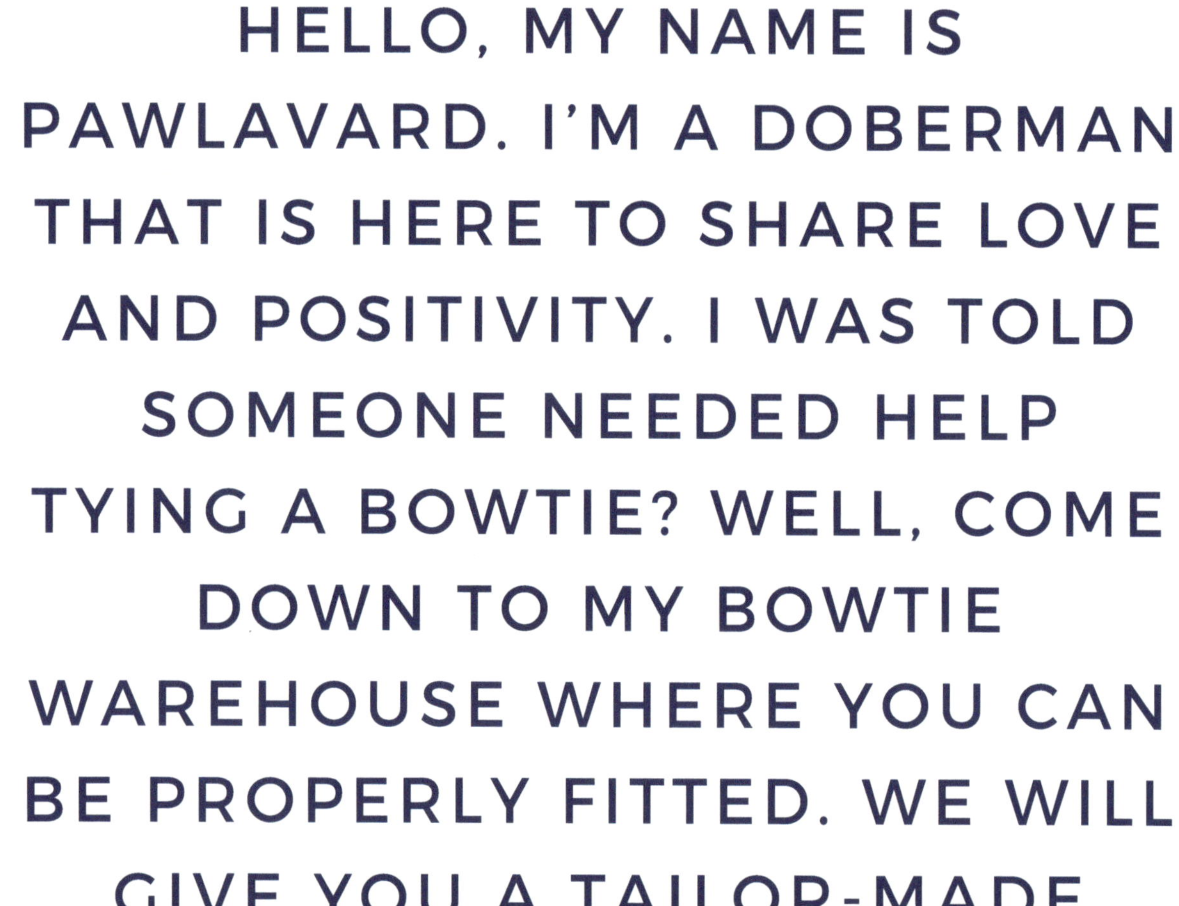

HELLO, MY NAME IS PAWLAVARD. I'M A DOBERMAN THAT IS HERE TO SHARE LOVE AND POSITIVITY. I WAS TOLD SOMEONE NEEDED HELP TYING A BOWTIE? WELL, COME DOWN TO MY BOWTIE WAREHOUSE WHERE YOU CAN BE PROPERLY FITTED. WE WILL GIVE YOU A TAILOR-MADE BOWTIE (FABRIC AND SIZE OF YOUR CHOICE) TO FIT ANY OCCASION.

BACKGROUND AND INSPIRATION:
ONE SUNNY MORNING, I PREPARED MY SON FOR A CLASS PRESENTATION. I NOTICED SOMETHING, REED (MY SON) WAS NERVOUS ABOUT HIS PERFORMANCE AND DIDN'T FEEL CONFIDENT IN HIS PLAIN OUTFIT. THAT'S WHEN I HAD AN IDEA. I TOOK ONE OF MY FAVORITE BLUE BOWTIES AND TIED IT AROUND REED'S NECK. INSTANTLY, HIS EYES LIT UP, AND CONFIDENCE SOARED.

"WOW, PAPA THIS BOWTIE MAKES ME FEEL SO SPECIAL" REED EXCLAIMED.

THAT MOMENT SPARKED AN IDEA IN MY MIND. I THEN REALIZED THAT BOWTIES HAD THE POWER TO MAKE PEOPLE FEEL UNIQUE AND CONFIDENT. THEN I THOUGHT, "WHAT IF I COULD SHARE THIS FEELING WITH ALL MY FRIENDS IN THE TOWN?" THAT'S WHEN I OPENED <u>TIE-PHISTICATED</u> (A MEN'S WAREHOUSE FOR BOWTIES).

IT BECAME MORE THAN JUST A BUSINESS. I ALSO STARTED HOSTING BOWTIE-MAKING WORKSHOPS AT MY SON'S ELEMENTARY SCHOOL. I TAUGHT THEM HOW TO CREATE THEIR OWN UNIQUE DESIGNS.

NO MATTER HOW SUCCESSFUL MY BUSINESS BECAME, I NEVER FORGOT THE JOY OF SEEING MY FRIENDS SMILE. THAT'S WHY I CONTINUE TO MAKE EACH BOWTIE WITH THE SAME LOVE AND MAGIC THAT STARTED IT ALL.

WITH A LITTLE CREATIVITY AND A LOT OF HEART, EVEN THE SMALLEST IDEAS CAN MAKE A BIG DIFFERENCE. MY IDEA TO START MAKING BOWTIES NOT ONLY TRANSFORMED THE TOWN BUT ALSO TAUGHT EVERYONE THE TRUE MEANING OF CONFIDENCE AND INDIVIDUALITY.

TODAY IS THE DAY WE EMBRACE OUR POTENTIAL. TODAY IS THE DAY WE STEP INTO THE LIGHT OF OUR OWN POSSIBILITIES. EACH OF US CARRIES WITHIN US A SPARK, A UNIQUE FLAME OF BRILLIANCE THAT THE WORLD DESPERATELY NEEDS.

PROFESSIONAL APPEARANCE:

BOWTIES CAN MAKE YOU LOOK DISTINGUISHED AND PROFESSIONAL, ESPECIALLY IN SETTINGS WHERE STANDING OUT POSITIVELY IS IMPORTANT.

WEARING A BOWTIE CAN
DEMONSTRATE ATTENTION TO
DETAIL AND A COMMITMENT
TO LOOKING WELL-GROOMED
AND PRESENTABLE.

WEARING A BOWTIE CAN BOOST CONFIDENCE. IT SHOWS THAT YOU ARE COMFORTABLE AND SELF-ASSURED IN YOUR STYLE CHOICES.

BOWTIES CAN TEACH THE IMPORTANCE OF DRESSING APPROPRIATELY FOR DIFFERENT OCCASIONS.

SPREADING JOY AND

CONFIDENCE:

A BOWTIE AT A TIME

COME DOWN AND MEET US AT MY NETWORKING LOUNGE CALLED <u>BAR-CHELLA</u> THIS SATURDAY. IT IS A FUNDRAISING EVENT YOU WOULDNT WANT TO MISS.

BY THE WAY:

YOU ARE EIGHT STEPS AWAY

FROM TYING YOUR OWN

BOWTIE

STEP 1:

DRAPE THE BOWTIE:
START WITH THE BOWTIE
DRAPED AROUND YOUR NECK,
WITH ONE END SLIGHTLY
LONGER THAN THE OTHER.

CROSS THE ENDS:

CROSS THE LONGER END

OVER THE SHORTER END.

STEP 3:

TUCK UNDER: BRING THE LONGER END UP THROUGH THE NECK LOOP AND PULL TIGHT.

STEP 4:

FORM THE BOW: FOLD THE SHORTER END TO FORM A BOW SHAPE.

STEP 5:

DROP THE LONGER END

OVER THE MIDDLE OF

THE BOW.

SHAPE THE BOW: FOLD THE LONGER END BACK TOWARD YOUR CHEST AND PINCH IT TO FORM A BOW SHAPE.

STEP 7:

THREAD THROUGH: THREAD THE PINCHED END THROUGH THE LOOP BEHIND THE BOW.

ADJUST: TIGHTEN THE BOW BY PULLING ON OPPOSITE ENDS AND ADJUST AS NEEDED.

YOU HAVE
OFFICIALLY
LEARNED HOW TO
TIE A BOWTIE

NOW THAT YOU'VE
LEARNED HOW TO
TIE A BOWTIE,
LETS GIVE YOU A
CONFIDENCE
BOOST!

AFFIRMATIONS FOR YOUNG MEN

BE SURE TO SAY
THIS IN THE MIRROR

I AM WHO I SAY I AM

I WALK WITH

DETERMINATION

AND ENTHUSIASM

I AM A LEADER

I TREAT OTHERS

WITH KINDNESS

AND RESPECT.

I AM IN

CONTROL OF

MY OWN

DESTINY.

I AM A POSITIVE

INFLUENCE IN MY

ENVIRONMENT

BOWTIES ARE NOT JUST AN

ACCESSORY BUT A

STATEMENT OF STYLE,

CONFIDENCE, AND ELEGANCE.

SUITABLE FOR ALL AGES

FROM CHILDREN TO ADULTS.